Concrete Music

books by F. D. Reeve

poetry

In the Silent Stones

The Blue Cat

fiction

The Red Machines

Just Over the Border

The Brother

White Colors

non-fiction

Aleksandr Blok: Between Image and Idea

Robert Frost in Russia

The Russian Novel

The White Monk: an Essay on Dostoevsky and Melville

CONCRETE MUSIC

poems by

F. D. Reeve

for [illegible]
Very best
FD Reeve
May Day '05

PYNCHEON HOUSE
amherst

First published in 1992 by Pyncheon House,
6 University Drive, Suite 105, Amherst, Massachusetts, 01002.
Printed in the United States of America

Grateful acknowledgment is made to the editors of the following periodicals: "Concrete Music" and "View Over Soho" first appeared in *American Poetry Review*; "Come, the wet leaves whisper" in *Bean Feast*; "The Wolves" in *Linden Lane Magazine*; "Sunset in Cancer off Cape Ann" in *The Little Magazine*; "Pieces" and "79th Street Boat Basin" in *The Manhattan Poetry Review*; "Winter Woods" in a special chapbook edition of *The New England Review*; "The South Windows at Chartres" in *New Letters*; "Tonight we are old lovers" in *The New Orleans Review*; "I Am Short," "The Tall Tree," and "Winter View of New Haven" in *The New Yorker*; "Long-limbed, lithe and lovely" in *Occident*; "Life-size" in *Poetry: a Magazine of Verse*; "Angling" in the *New Broadside Series* of The Press at Colorado College; "Carving the Circle," "The harbor fog is lavender," "The picture of your love," and "Skirting the House" in *The Sewanee Review*; "Autumn gathers country losses" in *Western Humanities Review*; and "The Horses" and "A Pair of Gloves" in *The Yale Review*. "The Anthill" appeared originally in *The Blue Cat* (New York: Farrar, Straus & Giroux, 1972). Early versions of "Nightway" appeared in a festschrift for Paul Horgan, in *Kansas Quarterly*, and in a limited, fine edition by The Press at Colorado College.

Library of Congress Cataloging-in-Publication Data

Reeve, F. D. (Franklin D.), 1928 –
Concrete Music: poems / by F. D. Reeve.
p. cm.
ISBN 1-8811-1956-4. – – ISBN 1-8811-1972-6 (pbk.)
I. Title.
PS3569.E44C6 1992 92 – 6099
811' .54 – – dc20 CIP

for Lenny

CONTENTS

SEASONS IN THE MIND

SEASONS IN THE MIND

There are four seasons in the mind of man
- Keats

I

In the mountains of her perfect self
nobody dies.

Spring dances on her velvet hair.
At dusk the sun flies

like the swifts up the valley, over the pass
into her white

porcelain and fantastic arms.
Heaven's light

contracts—a waterfall of glass.
Blue and above

the perfumed darkness, the moons of her eyes
shake with love.

*

Fog like mustard streaks the ground;
    silence, save the sound
    of heavy water.
Orion is nearly north now

pulled by the undertow
of the derelict sun.

How bright the heavens.
They pulse to your gentle guitar
and the pitch of your voice.

Like a widow disbursing bereavement,
wind wandering the pavement
scatters the news.

The stars cut off your fingertips.
No feeling in the lips.
This last act,

a coincidence of time and place,
is all. Suddenly your face
in late winter thaws.

On Mary's birthday, immaculate friend,
make the night end,
retouch the light.

*

How many times I have begun a letter
only to stop before the second word
has dried. In the silence, your not being here
is not being at all, though when I speak
(as when I play music) I think completely of you.
I imagine you listening. What you see, I believe,

is the essence of loveliness. If we meet,
will you write? I have not had a letter for days.

*

Happiness shines in your blue eyes
as the sun rises behind Red Mountain.
Night flees undisguised
down the long valley
past the stone fountain.

Far away, an archipelago
of clouds limns the horizon.
Dharma crowns life:
Fresh snow on the peaks
of the Sangre de Cristo.

High and clear, Lost Man Lake
mirrors the oyster moon.
Morning lifts the body;
your smile of light
bends and breaks.

*

Long-limbed, lithe and lovely a red fox
cuts a corner of the unleaved covert
into full view.
"Gone away!"
shouts the huntsman.

Wind rises.
The pursuit founders.

In a long dream of spring I see a fox
loping like light on the crowns of the covert.
Over her shoulder,
a mile behind,
my heart thunders.

II

By the sea I found an ammonite.
Its soul had gone, if one may say so,
but still the spiral held: rolled
in sand, my heart is an ammonite.

*

To you, lady, I doff my tan cap
(I am of a double life now proud)
which I have religiously put on—
(Much ring-kissing, love-making on clouds)
I stitch the sky to its bright peak—
(Loose as the wind, no dissent)
in real life the winter sun turns blue
(The mind's dark is heart's content)
and rain fills my cap like love.

*

The picture of your love is a round figure—
the perfect, lost circle a mystic would say,
like the silver ring on your fourth finger.
April floats lovers like birds, carries to sea
the winter's snow, old clouds, dried broken spray.
You are the water's music—flood and release.

You bend in the wind of desire like a tall willow;
old soft-banked river knows the ancient way;
snakes sleep in the sun as if they, too, had made love.
In May the air you walk through fills with swallows.

*

I am short. I cannot stop
the lilac clouds going over
the horizon. They slip

past my fingertips like wind
through my shirt. I once kissed
your face. Now in my mind

the eyes whiten, the outline blurs,
as twilight sits on a window sill
half in, half out of, doors.

If I were tall, I would turn
with the world. The moon would rise and set
on my palm. Your face would warm

like a glen of happiness. I would be free

to net all the white fish in the sky.
My fingers would swim through the sea.

*

Tonight we are old lovers.
You cradle my head and smile
on top of the covers (as if I
were a boy wheedling a kiss)
then peel back the dark.
The house shines with light
long after we part.

III

As from a mountain spring
clear water curls across
a granite stone
and beads from the lip in late July,

so in my summer mind,
palms against the sky,
you draw your perfume
like a ribbon across the olive landscape.

Your wet body in the sun
shines like a bird
embossed on the air.
In the wind your fingers dip the branch.

*

The sun leans on the ivory lids of your eyes
like a casual stranger. Flowers in your hair,
your hair becomes flowers. I whom your lips surprised
built this house of air.

If you rose literally out of the landscape today,
I would eat you, lick your mouth like candy, bind
your loose hair with the light that shakes the wind.
Look, a leaf moves: you are everywhere.

*

The harbor fog is lavender,
the sun is yellow salt;
the boats at anchor face the South
in summer thought.

Tall sky, tall flame: the eye wheels over
the salt-lipped edge of the sea.
Then the light breaks like loosening thunder
in the mind's eternity.

Beautiful this water music—
pure form and time in space—
as once Odysseus heard the Sirens
in an imaginary place.

*

Come, the wet leaves whisper. I slip to you
naked through knee-high grass. We touch in summer
with such phosphorescent rapture that our skins
glimmer like milk glass. You are blue and warm
with animal pleasure where your eyes and the stars meet.
The sky collapses, out of breath, then proudly
regains, expands, uplifts its empty self
as if to say there is no nature here
but some thin vacuum which by imperfection
holds the ceiling up. Close enough:

Who we really are we never know.

My thoughts are all-summer thoughts: in the sun
your gold hair like cornsilk smelling of hay;
your brown body bare on my palm.

*

The colored world reflected in your eyes
    is a lengthened vowel gone wild.
  Late summer hangs down like a y;
    the grapes are ripening.

We drink our tea from Chinese-patterned porcelain,
    laugh at foreign words
  while autumn overtakes the garden
    and ships unburden.

Like late-arriving light or the precessed moon,

you are not where you are.
I imagine the path to fame and fortune
is the road to the harbor.

From island to island across an empty sea
bent news of love takes time,
redder where the stars recede,
hottest where dying.

IV

Autumn gathers country losses:
windfalls rotting on the ground,
leaves, dead spirits' changelings—ghosts
and saints—spooked heads All Hallows' Eve—
the timorous accommodation to fact, not of.
Love sinks a little as each year comes round.

The moon draws up the world's lost music.
I hear it in the sea or under
a cliff where the water cracks like glass beads. The wonder
is that each wave is always first.

*

Above the cold sweet body of a river
a calf's bones lay like plastic glued to the rock
where they fell. The Old Forgiver

abandoned them. When you fell, did He grant you
a taste of the Tree of Life? To long for grace
    when we lie not touching the river

is to lie in small white pieces forever.
All composites dissolve, like two lovers.

*

Flies swarm on the living
    as well as the dead,
licking the sweat from the temple,
    the hot beads
of rain that lip from the eye.
    I hear your breathing,
desolate stone, as dry
    as Mount Lugnaquillia
whose heavy night wind
    batters the bracken.
Cuchulain, maker of hills,
    is gone, and Deirdre;
your body of love, removed
    to another time.
The flies from the wet dung rise
    in a remorseless hiss
through the failing light to embrace us
    as we climb.

*

Five hundred years: here.
        Not there.
Oxymorons the mode: flames
        lift raw
wet words—ALGOL the language
        of the Court.

Wings thunder. There, then there.
        The heart
shakes out five hundred years:
        dot dot dot.
Who blesses the black cross?
        Not here.

At last we are all last.
        Descends
then fear shaking the night.
        No love.
No error. Nothing. No waste.
        No body.

In the rigid frame framed death
        longer
than stillness, beauty's end,
        the alien
moment fired in her glazed
        eyes.

Immortality back; juniper

        in bloom—

the stiff, wooden petals
        of fame.
Straw lips, clay eyes waiting:
        not flesh

fish nor fowl. Dead.
        Not there.
Words on the bush burned:
        either / or:
who chose to stand watch
        here.

*

Stop. Look back. The times elide.
Foreshortened, years of childhood weave
between our legs like a selfish cat.
Your image trembles on the wall
of my memory. The picnic in air:
you and I on stippled grass
smiling, naked; your white straw hat.

And then? The light has erased
the kisses, laughter, the scent of your skin
drying in sunlight after a swim.
I, too, have grown quiet, tame.
I drive slowly and fear dying.
If you hear, wave from your frame. Your face
flares like a candle and then dims.

NIGHTWAY

NIGHTWAY A poem presenting an imaginary performance of the Navajo nine day ceremony of purification, celebrating the role of the Diné – the people; remembering the long walk and the four year exile at the Huelte – or fort; and expressing the power of the semi-arid open range – the Halbát-ha – to Navajo geography as fact and myth, and to some customs and traditions of the people seen in relation to Western cultural ideals and actual history

As a heron tiptoes
through water
on buckled legs
pecking the air
so
the **DODI-GOD**
pebbles the **HOGAN**
"dod, dod, doD, **DOD...**"
dod, dod, dod, dod...
shaking his fingers
like shills of corn.

Entrez, entrez:

TALKING-GOD & FEMALE,
the Melon of Imagination
&
the Red Plum,
hackles flecked with PAprika,
scatter
petals of
morTALity.
"OYEZ! OYEZ!"
shrieks the jay;
the KAIBAB squirrel
notes down in KAIBAB
o deceived barbarians!

how to transcribe

the joy of release
or whatever if any.

HE will—

yes,

one takes notes.

YES.

HE will
ora pro nobis

recover
in triplicate

what is

looped around

LIFE;

the 12 hoops

pressed on the **BODY**

stain

the skin.

a dozen glasses on a table
leach a dozen rings.

the bones wrinkle

& erode;

GUILT

is a broken hand
guilt is a broken hand

slapping the wAter.

ancestors sway

like dry wheat.

At dawn
dawn
dawn
dawn

the demons toss & turn;

the earth

sweats

with **FEAR;**

fingers
like cotton drumsticks

swab the air:

the **MASKS**

floating on the twilight

boil up in the stink,

suck the **BLOOD**

from cheeks,

lips,

from speechless adobe eyes.

A nose;

a hand

hooked in the dark,

bellowing;

a tongue

curling in flame

like a piece of yellow paper:

the **BODY**

repeats
repeats repeats repeats

its **LIFE**

in **PAIN,**

the PAGE

to which each reader returns
returns returns returns

who has lost

the thread

or

dropped the words.

DINÉ
DINÉ DINÉ DINÉ DINÉ DINÉ

wraps the mountain

in its arms.

The Tewa called them ÁPACHU,

the enemy
&

stranger,

one—

at Troy Achilles
chased himself three times
around the walls
before
he hacked great Hektor down;
then
Priam's city burned,
so forth
& so on.

The house of the dead

burned

for **DINÉ's**
DINÉ's DINÉ's DINÉ's
sake

who killed his horse,

pulled down his wall

&

tricked his spirit

into

oblivion.

O BELOVED CHINLEE!

Watch the noble warrior

fall;

Look:

the clouds—

a fanfare of wind.

The leather feet accelerate;

the plumed wands

are on his body;

he is rising

no more huelte

no more huelte

HE is in the yellow sunlight

& his body

his tongue

his eyes

is white.

The dancers

round the mounds of soil,

CORNBEETLE GIRL
&
POLLEN BOY

the patient

flattens the mountains of joy,

hail & farewell,

valley of joy,

there she goes down

with the one-legged boy,

down in the valley

of cinders.

The wind explodes

from over the mountain;

two hands blindfold the sun:

the golden

ÁPACHES DE NABAHÚ

mount the world:

in the dark

their testicles

thunder through the canyons,

their phalli

perforate the **HALBÁT-HA,**

the ox-tongued mesa

licks men's eyes,

&

mescal lays its

imitation
love-mask

of 1000 pieces

over 1 thick face.

The hands stiffen.

The penis goes limp.

Disease

like a rabbit

nibbles the heart.

MONSTER-SLAYER

weaves his magic

past the black drum

&
shrill knife

into the lesions of

DINÉ,

the holes
on the hummocked desert,

through the mud eyes
of the ancient **HOGAN**

&
the small loves
of blind
terrified old men.

Dawn returns on the **SUN's**
rewinding.

The **GIRL**

&

The **BOY**

are rebuilded by

hands of song,

& the

dance

rebegins

for the **BODY**

that cannot sing

or

dance long.

The days repeat

repeat repeat

for the dying **MASKers**

their mock pursuit of

HUELTE's wrong.

The **SHADOWS.**

LIFE is a... NO.

Over the green-gray land

the magic lantern

casts a... STOP.

Who can believe it?

The motheaten bison

the stoned squaws

alike

are tourist attractions.

Weaving rugs

against starvation

is madness.

The DISPOSSESSED are deaf & dumb,

the sheep are ravenous,

the pot-bellied agent is greedy,
&

The **DINÉ**

nods as if dead.

The garnisht tree no pendant stird,
No voice was heard of anie bird.

Who are these unbodied heads

sniffing at the cornmeal?

GODS have forebearance

pedigreed
moral

but this cardboard?
Canst dance out the eyes?

Who pokes his stick in the corn, faggot?

DANCE!

Employment is music,

the drum of the stolen pueblo,

erotic revival of

bone ash
&
buffalo dung.

MONSTER-SLAYER

scissors the

MASK:

the scraps

fall

like dry leaves,
&

eyes

shucked of pain

skip

HEAVENward

over the scorched plateau.

The earth is brown leather.

The feet drum in morning

after morning

Drums & Soldiers. Flourish. Alarums.

news of the night.

Tassels shake

between the FROGlegs:

No Man voids

his gift

aux mots de la tribu,

the community of defensive love.

Prayersticks in cornmeal:

feeding the MASKS.

Songs nourish the coyote.

In the sky-mirror

the universal face;

hands clamp shoulders,

ankles—

iron hands

hold a man in place.

But I have seen enough to know
that in this land I seem a dream,
& I feel ashamed of my own name.

Sand runs from an old man's fist

as from a broken hourglass.
In sand
on the leather floor
he paints
the metaphor,
the talking figurine.
It mocks the hot air,
blows the smoke to the ceiling,
spins the men to undress
whose heads
whirl like pinwheels.
The tips
of their feathers
stipple the walls
with **GRIEF**.

Wheeled like a wooden horse to test
the war,
the starved **PATIENT** staggers
through the doorway,
his sides heaving,
sweat clotting his neck,
his watery hands outstretched,
riffling the rancid air.
Down from the wooden hills
to the forked-stick hogans,
the horses,

the sheep,
stolen

the Spanish girls
slaves traded for horses

the **PATIENT** reweaves

the ultimate exercise.

He leaps

the wall of himself

into his **PEOPLE**,

weeping

for JUSTICE,

then crumples,

drunk,

onto his conscience.

Faster
fast fast fast fastfastfaster
the DRUMS.

Quick

the GODS'
reprisal

who surely measured out the red bayeta
& the pinon canyons of summer love,

whose vengeance purged DINETKA,
razed the stone cities,
rode the long-maned horses to the Rio Grande.

Always

the sens plus pur

the self-policing ritual

the primal story,
motive sans motion,

SNOW

on the San Francisco peaks.

Voices come to me from childhood;
the **DINÉ** speaks:
my unmasked
FRIENDS
surround me
like a lakeful of trout
quivering in bronze silence;
my hand
in the morning sunlight
opens the land
as if opening a door;
i see
the sinews
of distant thunder,
hear the clouds
ricochet off Mount Taylor.
A cicada
scrapes a lost tune.
Larkspur
&
blue flax;
phainopepla;
scorpions under the aspen,
in the wash—
universal electricity.

A herd of wild horses

canters across

the **HALBÁT-HA.**

A mountain lion

from Sierra La Sal

follows the dust.

The **MASKS** are moving in the SAND.

Friendly faces

coach the hands,

but these stiff,

initiated outlines

wobble rejection.

Not they

sign

the **NEW LIFE:**

it is

handspun & baize
blue & red

which a woman weaves

into her most beautiful blanket.

By the cloverleafed highway

the last horse

condemned

to the vultures—
bypassing bride-price

his topaz eyes

shine in the sunset.

A chromium truck

yaws toward Black Mountain.

The **LONG WALK**

to the HUELTE reversed,

pomegranate flowers
&

naja

in silver,

the shepherds cried,

"LET US GO HOME!"
"LET US GO HOME!"

& so

the moons of their eyes

rose

in the grandfather clocks

of the PAINTED DESERT.

Now

they lie assimilated,

drunk,

reflected

in a chip of glass

in the moonlight

by the roadside.

On the 8th day

the **WONDER-WORKER**

in a tattered

MASK

lashes

the people

out

of their pain.

SHOOTING GOD

scourges

the **DINÉ**

with word-bullets.

The whip purges

the velveteen **PEOPLE.**

Released,

the **PATIENT**

releases his

FRIENDS.

The year goes down

the mouth of the GOAT;

3 to 1—they sheared the range white

&

the drunk

staggers **HOME**

to his trinkets.

40 fingers feel the ultimate night.

Seeds burst from the SUN.

TALKING GOD stalks

the silence.

The 4 corners

of the round earth,

the 4 seasons
the 4 winds
circle
in front of the **HOGAN.**
2 HERONS
in love
do-si-do
in the doorway.
10 MASKERS
enter,
each a finger,
each a healer
toting up
the **DINÉ's** value,
the bridal **HOGAN,**
the tabooed mother
&
the fire of madness:
THE HERO in the **EAGLE's NEST**
vs.
THE SADDLE LEANED ON THE DOOR.
The spirits
come out of the paintings,
out of the sand
&
the earth-womb
led by

The CLOWN
under
The WAR-GODS.
Bare to the fire
with magic power
their purple bodies
sanctify
the helpers
&
the husbands,
all
whom **DINÉ** shelters
until death.

At dawn
on the 10th day
as the sun
reaches over
the Eastern mountains,
the purified
HOST
pays the
performers.
The **MASKS,**
like expired clouds,
vanish
into the turquoise air.

"We have neglected our ceremonies…

a dozen glasses spin like clockwork
in the bottling plant of the imagination

…therefore, the grass will not grow."

in the land of indifference the fields
are asphalt & the trees are stone

Who comes HOME
again
&
again
by the Ancient Way
that no longer
has meaning
to the empty house
that can never be cleansed
here
meets
the brown eyes of DEATH
&
the hypocrite's
folded hands.
He lets the ritual
wash over him
&
goes down
with his lust
in the wet dawn.

CONCRETE MUSIC

THE TALL TREE

She has the tall compactness of a tree
whose branches lift the evening air,
shouldering, like a trout its slippery green weeds,
the heavy desire always there.

The winged seeds tremble at the smallest change,
spin purposely to the soft lawn
like spiders weaving a geometry of chance,
flat shadows longing to be round.

In the waterfall of sky the black limbs
touch the new leaves to the stream.
(On his long walk through the dark Dante
shone with a light he had not seen.)

It stands as if on the edge of timeless space
in my memory, this tree in the garden:
How starry it gleamed last winter when the ice
froze around it like a glove.

WINTER WOODS

There is not silence in the woods
but winter arrangement of things.
Listen: wind drives the unanchored clouds
across the open sea.
The heavy maples crib and back.
Through the black rigging of branches
crows curve along the snow
  like Dutch women cleaning.

Figures in wood, but for the wood
not figures: Itself in Things:
if one could navigate salt clouds
or bend sail on a bent sea.
Like hanged bodies dry leaves swing back
and forth with the crows on the branches.
Imagine the white shadows of snow
  on the eyes, too, the cold cleaning.

Voices of silence inhabit the woods
like the terrible breaking of things.
High above earth, the changeable clouds
keep daily track of the sea.
After love, no looking back.
Friends' faces sway from the branches;
Persephone calls through the honeyed snow
  the news of spring cleaning.

SUNSET IN CANCER OFF CAPE ANN

What in the green world is lost when day
provides entry to evening? I cannot tell
the time or circumambulate the sea.
The sunshine sets the timid moon on fire.
Beetles swim the fields from night to night,
devouring the cloths in which they die.

Is this the last island of the earth to die?
I have imagined one more every day.
Children, who hold the candle in the night,
if there be something you still want to tell,
whisper it now before my hands catch fire
and melt on the surface of the red-lava sea.

The waves are round and moving. Will the sea
push and pull them flat? the moon, too, die?
Its only mansion is this death-by-fire
not bright enough to see what built the day.
From one phlegmatic sign can you foretell
the fortunes of dark planets in the night?

So many lies have fingered me at night
that I now dream of being lost at sea.
Cool, feminine and moist The Crab? I tell
you, more solace for a man about to die
would be a love on the edge of the lingering day,
a drink of water, then a kiss like fire.

From the breaking body bursts the last fire.
Faith flees from eyes in the black night.
(Broken fingers speak no language.) Day
after day the sun has shrunk until the sea
can swallow its crimson spot. Now as I die
I deny what I had thought to tell.

And, friend, forgive me. The stories we might tell
about making love would eat the fields like fire,
unbelieved by all who are in line to die,
but I am unready for the stars at night
and for this cool wind breathed by the cold sea.
On the tips of your fingers walks the light of day.

On the last day there is nothing left to tell.
The salt sea stops heaving, and our love of fire
blackens the night. Alone in their shells the crabs die.

VIEW OVER SOHO

1

Hard the steerage west;
harder being left behind.
The Cossacks wolfed the villages,
terrorized the mind.

Hardest the Holocaust:
the burned ghettos, like bones,
are ashes of lost years,
dry blood on German stones.

2

On Essex Street the cucumbers dance
in barrels of brine like yellow fingers.
Gray herring swell in the East River.
A girl held a mirror to look over her shoulder;
possible partners then waltzed to her hand;
she turned to pick one, and the rest, like boats,
swung downstream and were lost forever.
In stiff black hats and curly hair
their ghosts line the river. On the sabbath they march
up Hester and Leonard into a dream
of fresh air and a bath and a room of one's own
far from the Brooklyn Bridge. On Sunday
they polish the silver face of the past.
At night their eyes sparkle like diamonds.

The world of the old ideas, its tail
between its legs, slides along Grand.
    Few now draw the many to God's love.
The nine orders of angels have admitted
the unassimilable Jew.

3

Everything in the picture is brown.
The Lower East Side is being renewed.
Huge red trucks cart the *stetl*
up Fifth Avenue into the sunlight.
The herring are washed in soda water.
Losses and old loyalties,
like the Star of David, hide in the blue sky.
Row after row, the Philistines come first.
The East River shines without promise. Its hands
feel the shadows of suffering, the edge
of old age, the breaking city stones.

4

The careful buildings are silent.
Above their glass and limestone walls
stand the beautiful, painted stars
toward which each man makes passage,
which bear in their round wisdom
the shape of the universe
and its once constant light.

CARVING THE CIRCLE

Aries

Lady of violet and primrose,
born last, loved first, sprung
from the land by the cold rain,
bend my sword into a shadow
and let the steel shine on your breasts.

Taurus

Bachelor's buttons in May;
the proud bull charging, falling;
the matador shouldering the sun:
as the beautiful comes there comes violence
drawn by two heavy horses.

Gemini

Sixty-nine lovers? A mirror.
Midsummer Night flies upside-down.
I praise the two-backed beast,
stories of delight and the masks of love:
the future floats out of its egg.

Cancer

The trees in their summer dress;
the heavy footprints of heat;
the lake shimmering with love;
and by the verandah an oriole calling
to swimmers in the air.

Leo

The August lion holds hope
like a honeycomb in its white bones.
Alpha Leonis
is night's celebrity, the double star
whose green eyes scan the world.

Virgo

Sweet epithets become the fall:
queens in their honeyed crowns
turn gold before the frost.
Earth's iron heart draws the sun
toward the Southern Cross.

Libra

Stacked corn in full moon. Too cold
for a lark. The diminished season:
the trees hurry to grow old.
The ocean ebbs and floods,
keeping distinguished balance.

Scorpio

As the sun drowns, when night rises,
the soul sails out like the Ark
beyond the gardens of Ararat
and charted waters to the dark space
marked: Here Be Dragons.

Sagittarius

Hope gone; Chiron wounded;
the immortality passed on:
caged in the stars with our animals,
we circumstance our fate—
charred hands on the cave walls.

Capricorn

The lost light comes up late;
the lake makes a cirque in the snow;
dried currants in a silver bowl
like wooden drops of blood
stain the milk-glass sky.

Aquarius

An old woman hauling water
up from the well of her birthdays
breaks off a piece of heaven,
as bold as a barefoot girl in love
bearing her children home.

Pisces

Fish clap the water like hands
dancing as they lie dying.
Imagine the double helix
turning to fertilizer, the wild spin
till the body is hard and fast.

79th STREET BOAT BASIN

Sunday lovers come down to the river
in old wet shoes, their faces bright
with each other. They watch the gray ice shiver
against the spiles, the cold light carry
the frost-white yachts off into summer.
Flowering shrubs sway up and down like children
as if water and moon were swinging and drumming.
Their branches are spotted with burned-out cars.
As dusk falls, their petals flutter like eyes,
and the glass-skinned city turns gold. In the spring night
a thousand ships make love on the marble sky.

See Fat Lady Night turn tricks in the air
with the Hungry Stars! Stop at the Circus Delights
up ahead! Have a swim in the Genuine Dead Sea!
He who sets out on his heart's desire
believes the wind and tide are always fair.
So, come down tonight with me to the river, love.
From the dark we'll take the full rise of the dawn
and grow into a body of water
flecked with brown like anchors and old bones.
By day the yachts will bob on the surface like flowers,
and where we walk the sun will warm the stones.

PIECES

I'm thousands. Discounted forty percent,
I'm a warehouse of discontent,
old sofas speckled with dust, dead moths,
a stack of broken windows. Fortune spent,
I follow the ragpickers everywhere,
mouth turned down, eyes fixed and cold,
populating castles in the air.
It's all my fault:
    luck changes; love grows old;
    the red stripes of my heart flap in the wind.

If I left the darkness behind, as the dove
flew to happiness away from the Ark,
I'd follow your hands down the waves
of brown earth; I'd whirl up like a lark;
I'd turn into an idea of water, as fish
in a pond reshape the falling light;
I'd leap out of my skin like a clown at last brave
enough to mock burning and the small applause of the night.
    Then I'd tell you and the wind my last wish,
    how to unwrap the pieces of love.

CONCRETE MUSIC

The hunting horns that wound around
Chambord
the Bois de Boulogne
a stable of mistresses
blaring the king's desire
blasting the white oaks
bending the mud-footed peasant to heel
are now an orchestra of cars
forever circling Paris
like wingless angels,
night after night
jamming the square
in front of Saint Pierre.
Deaf and lonely
like the musicians of Bremen
in their willful cacophony,
vain and lusty
like Louis the Fourteenth
in his self-righteousness,
the drivers run over
each other
with noise:
not a leaf
left on a tree;
in the gray sky
after the rain
not a bird.

Blue pigeons pecking in the gutter
a tin fork scratching in a saucepan
a sudden mouse in a moonlit wall

    skim a shudder down the spine
    and turn the air colder
    like a draft or a siren: what? when?

Then the tall wooden doors are slowly rolled open
Then the garbage cans are scraped across the concrete
Then the sun crashes into the window

Swinging like a lily of the valley
        belled in its green bower
a little bride in white
        stops on the church steps
        under the Roman arch
to be taken once and for all
        photographed laughing

    lightslightslights
    her veil waves
    in his dark suit her husband stands dumb and proud

And the great bells in the clock tower
    ring their noon praise
    as everyone does
    for what's to be done

This is the song the deaf hear.

Saturday from Église Saint Pierre
bearing crowns of roses, a polished oak coffin
and two heavy-hearted women in black,
a hearse pulls into the Paris traffic.
The smell of death pours from the heavy bells.

By the door a beggar blows on his hands,
rubs them, warms them in his pants.
I think they're hidden like the bells,
the dead, a holy bit of Mary's veil,
young Joan's mad faith in saints and grace
or whatever's meant by "the spirit of France."

For me, too, these iron bells speak loss.
Their music splinters on the stones
like voices, shines like pieces of glass,
then slides down into the afternoon.
I pretend it means the weather'll change,
but nothing does. I can tell by my bones.

Once a body was a measure,
called a fathom six feet long,
but now everything's measured by light.
I can't feel the edge of outer space
or my own: the iron silence of the night
is shattered by the merciless bells.

The clouds bell from the West,
break along the clerestory rails

in wave after wave where the ogives
divide the stained glass,
then flood transept and nave
washing the altar like an island,
the air as black as the sea

high on the cold gray stones
bright squares of colored light

The music swells toward the East,
swerves toward the cross like a wild beast
slamming the earth, bellowing
its pride, tossing small lives to the wind,
thundering, shaking the trees,
the sky white from fear, all eyes blinded,
and below—the gasping sea

high on the cold gray stones
thin squares of colored light

Sweet, and sharp as glass,
one voice rises from the dark,
lifts off from the heavy breathing—
a cadenza, a trumpet of ecstasy,
a saint's melody, a paean
to presence praising us as we are
for love of what we become

high on the cold gray stones
pale squares of colored light

THE WOLVES

I read about torture in El Salvador:
about women stuffed with mice and marred by knives;
about men disemboweled alive and then dismembered;
about scraping maggots off childen's eyes with a spoon;
how drunken soldiers line campesinos up
to chop off their legs like cutting sugar cane.

Cursed Ugolino in Hell: my blameless friends
disbelieve as they watch him suck his son's bones
and blink from the wet corner like a rat.
Guilt holds them, half rich, tighter than chains.
Then out of the dark comes the hunchbacked faith
that suffering makes a man see through the stones.

Never. The heavens are an elaborate lie—
eccentric stars amused by their odd motions;
old dogs trying to couple in a public park.
More credible the void: nothing from nothing.

Like the gold coin that Ahab nailed to the mast,
each tortured body shines up ahead in the moonlight
on our quest for mercy from our terrible past.

At last the wolves close in. They rise like the wind
from regret, hungry, howling, not knowing the end
of one generation or if a next will begin.

LIFE-SIZE

Shellacking the water, ha! *That* a mirror?
Show and Tell. "Behold," the Old Forgiver
babbles again, "the Seven Wonders are moving."
My foot. The center is mad Virginia's lover
as tall and cool as Philadelphus' Pharos,
the blinking entrance, ithyphallic *foris*

which opens and closes as the water swirls
around its base and breaks in a million pearls.
I've watched stupid fish guzzle the foam
of that farina and pass out on the oxygen lawn,
the giant fellated by a school of friends
who suck the public ocean for private ends.

The great pizzle lifts, leaps, plunges in the sea;
waves grapple the groin; green water bleats,
boils; the red-mouthed bitch ululates
her passion to universal alleluia.
Her eye shines in the moonlight like broken glass;
his sperm sink in the Mariana Trench.

Each morning off Cape Hatteras they kiss,
the pinfish, reserving themselves a day's success.
To live life through, like hopping from island to island,
is small potatoes, the safe manoeuvers of airmen
who oil the young Pacific for fear of the waves
and fly above the lighthouse to watch the whales.

WINTER VIEW OF NEW HAVEN:
Yale College Towers, the Breakwaters and Stratford Shoal Beyond

The old tower shines like the Matterhorn;
snow melts on the intricate façade
of United Illuminating.

Below, the asphalt lot has been plowed.
The prize-winning moon mounts in the West
on a long, lavender cloud.

Albert Ryder might have painted this,
done justice (as historians say)
to the dead sky, the kiss

of ice on the harbor like purple glass.
Helen high on runaway love
lifts the white sheet to the past.

Symbols: Paris sleeps on black stones;
Priam's gold is gone; Hektor's blood
spots his broken bones.

Feel the wind on your cheek? It slips
through your fingers like water in a dream.
It drives proud ghosts like ships

into pennants of smoke
on a wine-dark sky.

A PAIR OF GLOVES

Look: no hands. The fingers curl back,
touching like lovers.
The knuckles fold into Chinese mountains;
fresh snow on the pines.
A leaf, a door, the shadows of feathers.

After a concert the walls hold the song,
release the story.
Lovers' losses pour down the mountain
of shadows like birds,
rise like light in blue weather.

THE HORSES

Mind if I walk around the abandoned farm?
In March shadows cant forward, longing for light.
At the back of the mind, under newspaper snow,
    crocuses finger our wet hands.
A cardinal whistles from the crown of the sugar maple
as if the sap were running up his legs,
    out his throat.

I remember the thighs and the smell of the proud horses
who charged from their stalls each morning at the fresh sun.
Their hoofs clattered across the marble washstand.
    They sank in the tall grass, as small
as a flock of crows on a green lawn. A boy
ran after them into the silence, the sweat of their leather
    on his hands.

I am blinded by sunlight. Who shifts behind the dark window?
I cannot feel the fish in the ocean. Birds
avoid my horizon on the way to their habitat.
    Nothing moves between the lines.
Painfully breath shortens near the mountain peak
where the sun bleeds on the granite and eagles and weasels
    drown like rats.

The twelve tents of the Zodiac are lies.
The sun on its knees goes around the world

looking backward forever, festering malice.
    The dead stars shift with the sand.
My window frames a lover or a fish
that burns with a scarlet flame. Even the leaves
    fall on that basis.

The light that passes through the lemon woods
holds our intact stars. Italic footnotes
like self-centered cats shadow the sentences.
    Goldfish nibble their fingernails.
Birds whirl in nebulae. The triumphant voice
is the call of the foam-flecked horses cantering
    into silence.

SKIRTING THE HOUSE

Our house stands by a brook at the edge of a wood,
between the brook and a dead-end road.
(Cars that go up five minutes later come back.)
Tables and chairs, lamps, pots, stove, books
wait at the walls through the night. At dawn
there's a window for everything we do.
When the trees are bare and the leaves lie brown
and curled in corners of the lawn,
and the gray air smells of snow,
it's time to skirt the house.
All around beneath the windows
we wrap black felt paper, nail a row
of rough fir lath on top like a belt,
pin the bottom with stones, so the melting
snow won't soak into the wood.
Every year we say we should
put up some sort of fence
to protect the glass against pebbles and ice
and to block the view of the neighbor's yard,
full of unfloatable boats and rusted cars.
He has one motor and a blue van that run.
Lying west of the road, he gets the morning sun
a half hour earlier. Then it must be hard
to see our house still couched in the dark,
a man and a woman sleeping under its skirt,
legs twined together as in the earth.

THE SOUTH WINDOWS AT CHARTRES

Night after night I dream
pictures of delight—
a tropical air throbbing with perfume,
parrots shrilling in tall palms,
sunlight green on a milky sea;

or the lush valleys of Lebanon
heavy with cedar
and the burnt-honey scent of new-mown hay
where white lilies on Easter morning
trumpet the Second Coming.

Climbing to ecstasy
each mind has visions,
as if on Forty-Second Street
Saint Teresa saw Adam and Eve
streak through the tinted sky.

ANGLING

The lake has buttons: I see
the islands button the water.

No waves near the islands,
no one sailing away.

An iridescent fish
threading wavering weeds

is compatible with green,
is the innocent wish.

Sunlight bobs on the surface,
hangs its hooks in the water,

itself hangs in the sky
threaded through empty space

like a fish pulled round an island
by the black hooks of hunger.

What is isn't real enough,
doesn't account for the silence

between clouds or the evening sky
or the wet weight of water,

or the last irresponsible splash
when the fish rises to the fly.

THE ANTHILL

THE ANTHILL

1

Old women in black hoods
shuffle in to pray for the dead.
(Ants store grain in special ground.)
Jesus rips his hands
free from the nails to touch their loins.
See where his blood has soaked the wood?
They kiss it. They press their cheeks against
the warm brown stains.
When infidels flooded
the fields and washed away the grain,
this white house of God, besieged,
shot up a brighter flame.
One spring the roof fell in;
Heaven itself shouldered the rain
until the cross rose higher still.
When Indians attacked, the pastor named
his flock "The Soldiers of God's Will."

The Church was the center of New England life

The Church was the leader of society.

Plimouth Colony experienced a double fate.

Winter huts, like saints in shrouds,
await the Easter resurrection.
Beggars crawl on hands and knees
around the relics of the nation.
Three shadows rise like crumpled bats,
three black-faced girls with outstretched hands

The Fates forever reenact mortality.

whirling up the groin of Heaven.
Across the floor in single file
the ants transport their packs of sin,
weeping freely toward the grail
filled with their loneliness. A sudden
silence blanks the wooden walls;
the wine boils up; and fear walks in.

2

At his birth who were present remarked
the oblong head, the spatulate fingers
instinctually weaving the smoky air;
praised John and Cynthia for a second son
to be a maker of pencils.
With his father's pencils he ruled the land,
"one of the finer American minds"
who took his time, like his people, in hand.
His ghost hangs on the wall:
as the winter fire dies down
and the winds blow across Walden Pond,
a hundred thousand men buy
seeds and sails, call for self-reliance,
and dream of a solitary empire
saluted by the red, morning sun.
With his father's pencils Henry David
has drawn circles around them, friends,

The lead pencils exhibited by J. Thorough & Co. were considered superior to all others.

Thoreau, baptized David Henry, lived from 1817 to 1862.

the forty-four stations of his life:
he left nothing to lament.

3

Father, fornicator, release me.
Ille vim tulit invitae.
Aut mihi redde meos
aut me quoque conde sepulchro.
Of my spare years what have I saved
that will free me in the city?
Saints beach icons in the spray
at Sandy Hook. Pity
drags the Fifth Avenue bus.
A thousand immigrants each Fourth of July
wash garbage, hoe water.
Convicted scholiast, once I
wanted Sewall's daughter,
wanted to bed a perfumed lady.
As a river, turned from its course,
ravages its way to the sea, so I braid
my career with what she refused.
My body is bad; that woman's worse:
she sparrows on brick words,
mindlessly foraging; love is a curse
in her dirty stone dead woods.
Hesper in the transcendent sky,
suck my hot eye.

Metamorphoses, IV, 240; VII, 618.

The more Thoreau saw New York, the worse he thought it.

Ellen Sewall's father prevented her marrying one of those radical transcendentalists.

4

Thoreau was careless with a campfire; subsequently he insisted that the flames merely consumed their natural food.

Flames from the pine stump
finger Fair Haven Pond:
three hundred acres, six
dressed trout burn.
Shamans slay the tinder
with orange tongues;
witches devour wood;
demons dare
the blind to fondle fish
on the boiling surface.
Dogs gnaw the leg bones
of civilized man.

5

First editor of *The Dial*, Margaret Fuller drowned in a shipwreck off Fire Island. Emerson asked Thoreau to search for her body.

Margaret Fuller was too smart.
She disapproved my rugged art.
"Too assuming," "badly bred,"
"Give it me again," she said.
Margaret Fuller is dead.

"I know the men of this countree,
and not a one is match to me.
They're ignorant, vain, easily led,
unsympathetic." That's what she said.
Now she's dead.

6

His voice trumpeted down the Merrimack,
thundered in the bad Concord air,
"speaking to their condition to make them wince."

Schoolteacher, lecturer, naturalist, land surveyor, he turned a two-week outing into his first moral epic.

"A man does best when he is most himself."

Teacher, he held his hands behind his back;
his lecturer's finger chid, then flicked his hair
from his forehead; he surveyed the Mount of Venus.

The land was his by labor and by measure.
"He who is right is a majority of one."

7

The ants jostle through the pews
toward their love, which burns in Heaven,
entitled *Holy*: The Many and The Few,
an ancient story author Herman
Melville knew but made his captains
sail and resail until the end,
as limp as a fall on a capstan,
flapping on the brass like a severed hand.
The priest who holds the Book of Prayer
mumbles absolution, death
by fire for the sins of air
fanned by an albatross's breath.

Thoreau told himself in his Journal that the effort to lead the life which a man imagines will bring unexpected success.

Worms and lovers of dark ways
greet death by water: there the font
washes the heart; the skin decays,
cast off by the soul; and plain men plant
complex redemption, stealing colors
from the funky chart of time. That blue
which from the Pacific pours into Walden
Pond becomes a pair of eyes
straining from the cold stone floor
to face above the Eucharist.
Age, like the wind, howls at the door,
but the believer, kneeling, shakes his fist,
then opens his hand for a cardboard wafer.
In a forest temple there are no pews;
death is neither later nor safer,
but a lover expresses no heretical views.
Free man devours himself alive
without devil or alternative.

He believed that a government always crucifies Christ.

8

False gods! Fear! Fear! Fear!
Stop!
Hath no man a painted paradise on his church wall
harpes et luthes
or where virgin receiveth message
Mr Adams or no

The Cantos of Ezra Pound,
XLV.

WITH USURA
between the bride and her groom
No!
The sword in the stone
No!
War stagnates
commerce falleth apart
estates separate
beds divide
clothes unstitch
bread poisons
Nor even the Indians
smallpoxed
could stand
CONTRA NATURAM
the dead dog on the hearth
the corpse at the table
on the pillow
a gray skull
papered over
with dollar bills.
Disobey.

**Unjust laws exist;
men must make the
law free, said Thoreau.**

9

Divine afflatus drove his desperation.

Thoreau's aunt reported that going to see Henry at Walden Pond was one of Concord's first recreations.

Goodness guided the grant of a house
in return for planting the forest. The rest
at cost would come by cart from Concord
like Joseph Hosmer and all whom Henry hosted
as the shingles over the cellar shaped
the hut into history's home. Two years;
then Master Ralph motioned his man,
Waldo the creditor won over Walden,
and the writer retreated who had never ranged far,
who had borrowed an axe to begin his building,
who had siphoned a style from the stiff lips
of the nation. Nobody needed that joke.
Fey philosopher of India, foister!

10

Courts were made for fair weather, wrote Thoreau, and for very civil cases.

Aristotle lied. By nature men
are summer friends. The history of slaves
shows that their bank and compass is *to have*.
The sun that gives each figure's fix at noon
takes away the shadow; conceit then says,
Thou art the Form, the earth, thy property.

Blind as slime mold, all together build
ameboid temples where they pray for grace,
unforethoughtful of the winter wind
which some brisk day will blow their skyscrapers
apart, befouling every place.

Immoral slave who pleads a moral cause,
bankrupt in Heaven and on earth a stone,
man sets his course against the natural laws,
plotting the steps to seize the beautiful
but coming, after all, to his own wet bones.

11

As a trout lurks in a quiet pool
contemplating the surface,
he swung deep inside his soul,
his "most sacred nature,"
conjuring society there,
the reaches of the river,
the unroofed book, the pantheist air,
triumph out of failure:
"I have now a library of nearly nine hundred volumes,
over seven hundred of which I wrote myself."

When his first book was remaindered, he bought all the copies.

"The horses came running, for company I thought."
Bent said I might put it in my book so,
it would do no harm, but in fact they came for salt.
There was some in my pocket, I replied.
Bent said, "That's what they smelt, the salt."

The lover humanizes: the naturalist follows.

12

In the dark corner of the nation
crawling through the shadows cast

A bad government makes life less valuable.

by lights from the capitol's dome, an impatient
black man tunnels out of the past
toward the altar of the North Star.

Today John Brown is hanging: Alcott
is reading the Bible; Emerson's part
is the text of the telegram; David
will quote applicable verse, later
dispatch a defense to the memorial
service in the Adirondacks.

The congregation prays for freedom
but cannot compensate its lacks
by making, or by giving the captured Indians,
Christianity and artifacts.

13

Thoreau met and admired Whitman, said that men had reason to be ashamed of themselves.

The beast will burst from the tin cage.
Its flames will burn the Latin words
of the ground-sniffer, will boil the collyrium
off his agate eyes. Its bared rage
will terrorize the queens of Concrd
and drive their white fingers to delirium.

14

He went to Minnesota in search of health.

La Riviere Longue rises
in the sunset.

Tubercular man aspires
to drink it,
to be purged and repaired
by water,
to cool the room's smoked air
and make the mind shine as
it ought to.

Death cuts a hundred lesions
in a lover.
A façade is cracked by collisions
with moving
wishes. Time is power.
His mission
turns cold and sour
who fears the ant's fundamental
passion.

He died of tuberculosis and was buried in Concord's Sleepy Hollow Cemetery.

This book was designed and set
in 11 point Goudy Regular by
Joan G. Letendre, and printed
by Daamen Inc.

Cover: The Duomo and the
Arnolfo Tower, Florence, from
an Alinari photograph c. 1890.

Pyncheon House logo by RAS.